GREECE

ABDO
Publishing Company

GREECE

by Marcia Amidon Lusted

Content Consultant
Gonda Van Steen
Cassas Professor in Greek Studies, University of Florida

CREDITS

Published by ABDO Publishing Company, PO Box 398166, Minneapolis, MN 55439. Copyright © 2013 by Abdo Consulting Group, Inc. International copyrights reserved in all countries. No part of this book may be reproduced in any form without written permission from the publisher. The Essential Library™ is a trademark and logo of ABDO Publishing Company.

Printed in the United States of America,
North Mankato, Minnesota
092012
082013

 THIS BOOK CONTAINS AT LEAST 10% RECYCLED MATERIALS.

Editor: Arnold Ringstad
Series Designer: Emily Love

About the Author: Marcia Amidon Lusted has written 70 books and over 300 magazine articles for young readers. She is also an assistant editor, a writing instructor, and a musician.

Cataloging-in-Publication Data

Lusted, Marcia Amidon.
 Greece / Marcia Amidon Lusted.
   p. cm. -- (Countries of the world)
Includes bibliographical references and index.
ISBN 978-1-61783-629-9
1. Greece--Juvenile literature.   I. Title.
949.5--dc22

2012946071

Cover: The island of Sými in southeast Greece

TABLE OF CONTENTS

CHAPTER 1
A VISIT TO GREECE

Your taxi winds its way through the maze of streets that make up the city of Athens. As you look up, you see the sun shining on the white columns of the Parthenon. It is perched on the Acropolis, a hill high above the city. The Parthenon is an ancient Greek temple and Athens' most famous landmark. Everywhere you go, you are reminded of the Greek culture that first existed here 4,000 years ago and

RESTORING THE PARTHENON

The restoration project at the Parthenon has already taken 30 years and $90 million. The effort is like trying to assemble a "20,000-ton [18,100 metric ton], 70,000-piece, three-dimensional jigsaw puzzle," according to the 2008 PBS television program *Secrets of the Parthenon*.[1] Workers are trying not only to reassemble the fragments of the buildings, which are scattered across the Acropolis and museums around the world, but also to undo the damage caused by less sophisticated restoration efforts in the past. The team uses computers to catalog all the fragments and determine where they originally fit. They must also fabricate new marble sections to replace those that are lost. At the time of *Secrets of the Parthenon*, workers estimated the project would be completed within 10 years.

The structure of the Parthenon was completed in 438 BCE.

has influenced so much of the rest of the world. Greece is where the system of government known as democracy developed. It is also the birthplace of the Olympic Games.

As you climb the slope of the Acropolis, you are walking on ground that was once said to be the province of the gods. It has also been a fortress and the site of a Byzantine church. When you reach the top, you pass through the Propylaea, the monumental gateway to the Acropolis. As you walk around the Parthenon, parts of which are being restored by archaeologists and conservators, you can see ancient Greek history all around you. Sculpted images of gods, goddesses, and mythological figures adorn the building. More fragments of the Parthenon's marble friezes can be seen in the New Acropolis Museum, located nearby. As you walk to the other side of the Acropolis, you are walking on the most sacred ground of the hill, where the Erechtheum temple is located. This is where the ceremonies of

DISMANTLING THE PARTHENON

Beginning in 1801 and continuing for several years, Thomas Bruce, Earl of Elgin, removed many sections of marble sculpture from the Parthenon, totaling almost half of the surviving original decorations. With the help of his wife, he took them back to England where they were later bought and displayed by the British Museum. For many years the Greek government asked to have the marbles returned to Athens. When the New Acropolis Museum opened in Athens in 2009, pressure increased on the British Museum to return the marble sculptures to Greece. There is even a British Committee for the Reunification of the Parthenon Marbles, which is working towards this goal.

A visitor looks at a display in the New Acropolis Museum. The empty space stands in for the statue from this collection that is now in the British Museum in London.

Poseidon and Athena took place. The Temple of Athena Nike perches on a platform at the edge of the Acropolis. Here, Athenians prayed for success in warfare. The word *Nike* means "victory" in Greek. On other parts of the hill, more remains of temples and theaters can be seen. You are surrounded by the legacy of ancient Greek architecture and ideas,

a legacy that has made its way all around the world and continues to inspire today.

A TWENTY-FIRST-CENTURY CITY

But Athens is also a modern, bustling city with a metropolitan area packed with more than 3 million people.[2] There are many cars and motor scooters, creating air pollution and sometimes making it difficult for pedestrians to safely navigate streets. Modern concrete and cinder block buildings exist side by side with ancient ruins. There are many small, distinct neighborhoods in Athens, and each one is similar to its own small city. Some areas are a patchwork of oddly shaped streets, the remnants of neighborhoods dating from before Greece achieved independence from the Ottoman Empire. More modern grids of streets span other parts of the city. Ermou Street stretches in a straight line from the parliament building—once a palace—past the foot of the Acropolis. But in some areas of the city, the modern architecture and congested streets could belong to any city in Europe.

Athens is the southernmost capital city in mainland Europe.

Athens is a tourist destination, and it has many sidewalk cafes and restaurants to entice visitors. Here you can try everything from gyros to lamb chops to sweets such as baklava. The central market features

Greeks and tourists walk through Monastiraki Square in Athens.

Political Boundaries of Greece

MACEDONIA
Skopje
BULGARIA
TURKEY
Tirane
ALBANIA
EASTERN MACEDONIA
AND THRACE
Kavalla
Komotiní
Alexandroupolis
Sea of
Marmara
CENTRAL
MACEDONIA
Thessaloníki
MOUNT
ATHOS
WESTERN
MACEDONIA
Kozáni
Gulf of
Thermai
Aegean
Sea
Ioánnina
EPIRUS
Corfu
Corfu
Lárissa
THESSALY
Volos
Sporades
Mytilene
NORTH
AEGEAN
Lesbos
TURKEY
Lamía
Agrinion
CENTRAL
GREECE
Delphi
Euboea
Khalkis
Chios
IONIAN
ISLANDS
Patras
WESTERN
GREECE
Corinth
ATTICA
Piraeus
Athens
Vári
Samos
Trípolis
Saronic
Gulf
PELOPONNESE
Hermoúpolis
Sparta
Ionian
Sea
Cyclades
SOUTH
AEGEAN
Rhodes
Dodecanese
Islands
Rhodes
Sea of Crete
Khania
CRETE
Iráklion
Mediterranean Sea

International boundary
Regional boundary
National capital
Regional capital
City or village
0   50 Miles
0   50 Kilometers

NORTH

everyday needs, such as meat and produce, as well as clothing and souvenirs for tourists. In other parts of the city, expensive boutiques offer designer clothing and crafts.

As dusk settles in, the lights of the city come on. On the Acropolis, spotlights turn the white walls and columns of the ruins a golden hue, glowing above the glaring lights and neon of modern Athens.

THE OLD AND THE NEW

Greece is a land balanced between past and present and between the bustle of its cities and the rural flavor of its highlands. Some parts of the country feel focused on its history, such as the ruins at Delphi or the remains of the original stadium of Olympia, where many events in the ancient Olympic Games took place. In these areas you can explore the land and mythology of the ancient Greeks. In other places, such as the islands of the Aegean Sea, you can relax and enjoy beautiful scenery and beaches. Whitewashed houses, windmills, and monasteries dot the landscape. In the mountains of Greece, you can discover beautiful lakes, rivers, and forests, and perhaps glimpse a wild ibex, a bear, or a fox. The region of Thrace bridges eastern Europe and Turkey; Greek Orthodox churches and Muslim mosques exist side by side. Thessaly, on the Aegean coast, is one of the most beautiful parts of Greece. Delphi is set in a dramatic landscape of mountains that look out over the Corinthian Gulf. No matter what sort of landscapes or

There are more than 50 museums in Athens alone.

activities you like, there is a region of Greece where you can find them.

Behind its rich history and beautiful landscapes, Greece struggles with modern issues. It is a country suffering from severe economic troubles, pollution, and political instability. As part of the European Union (EU), Greece has benefited from cooperation with neighboring countries. Fellow EU nations extended loans and bailout money to Greece during the worst of its economic crises but also imposed extremely strict austerity measures. Greece had a great deal of work to do to overcome its challenges, but the Greek people were up to the task.

"We are all Greeks. Our laws, our literature, our religion, our arts, have their root in Greece."[3]

-Percy Bysshe Shelley

SNAPSHOT

Official name: Hellenic Republic

Capital city: Athens

Form of government: parliamentary republic

Title of leaders: prime minister (head of government), president (chief of state)

Currency: euro

Population (July 2012 est.): 10,767,827
World rank: 78

Size: 50,949 square miles (131,957 sq km)
World rank: 97

Language: Greek

Official religion: Greek Orthodox

Per capita GDP (2011, US dollars): $27,600
World rank: 49

CHAPTER 2

GEOGRAPHY: A LAND OF SEAS AND MOUNTAINS

Greece is a relatively small country, less than 51,000 square miles (132,000 sq km) in size, but it has many regional differences packed within its borders. Three seas surround Greece: the Mediterranean Sea to the south, the Ionian Sea to the west, and the Aegean Sea to the east. Across the Ionian Sea lies the country of Italy, while Turkey is located across the Aegean Sea. Greece is bordered on the north by Albania, Bulgaria, and the country of Macedonia (which, due to an ongoing name dispute, Greeks refer to as "the former Yugoslav Republic of Macedonia," or FYROM). Greece occupies the tip of what is known as the Balkan Peninsula.

One-fifth of the country is made up of small islands scattered throughout the Ionian and Aegean Seas. There are thousands of

Skorpios Island is one of Greece's thousands of small islands.

these islands, but only approximately 170 of them are inhabited. In Greek mythology, the gods known as the Titans tore the tops from the Greek mountains and the pieces fell into the sea, creating the islands. You are never far from the sea when you are in Greece. Even on the mainland, no one lives more than 60 miles (37 km) from the coast.

GREECE'S REGIONS

There are nine regions on the Greek mainland (Attica, Central Greece, Central Macedonia, Eastern Macedonia and Thrace, Epirus, Peloponnese, Thessaly, Western Greece, and Western Macedonia) and four island groups (Crete, the Ionian Islands, the North Aegean, and the South Aegean). These 13 regions were once divided into 54 smaller divisions called prefectures, but they were abolished in 2011. Today the regions are divided into 325 municipalities instead.

Greece's biggest cities are located along the coasts. This includes its largest city, Athens, where almost a third of the Greek

population lives. Athens is located in the Attica region on the eastern coast of the Greek mainland. It has a population of 3.25 million people, although the uncertain size of the immigrant population may boost this significantly.[1] Thessaloníki, Greece's second-largest city, is located in the Central Macedonia region and has a population of 834,000 people.[2] Another major city is Patras, the capital of the Peloponnese region, with a population of just over 170,000 people.[3] Its location on the Ionian Sea makes it an important port for ferries to Italy and the Ionian Islands. Other large cities include Iráklion on the island of Crete, with approximately 138,000 people, and Piraeus, a port city of nearly 176,000 near Athens.[4]

LOOKING AT THE LAND

Most of Greece consists of mountains and peninsulas. Because there are so many peninsulas and islands, Greece has approximately 8,500 miles (13,500 km) of coastline— nearly as much as China.[5] The largest mountain range is the Pindus, which runs north

THE CAVE AT VÁRI

Vári, on the Attic Coast of Greece near Athens, is the home of a cave that contained many ancient artifacts dating from the fifth century BCE. Inscriptions and sculptures, some of them parts of shrines or temples, are carved right into the cave's walls. A team of US archaeologists excavated the cave in the early twentieth century, and some of its artifacts are now in museums.

to south through the central mainland. The highest point in Greece is the summit of Mount Olympus, famous from Greek mythology as the legendary home of the gods. Greece's mountains also include dormant and active volcanoes such as Santorini, Methana, and Nisyros. All of Greece's volcanic mountains are located in the southern islands.

Less than one-third of the land in Greece is suitable for agriculture.[6] Crops include tobacco in the northeast, cotton in the central mainland, and fruits and vegetables in the south. The rest of Greece's land is mountainous; not only is the mountain terrain difficult to live on, but it also has thin, rocky soil with limestone outcroppings, where plants do not grow well. Some of the land that is good for farming has a kind of clay soil called *terra rosa*, or reddened earth, which comes from the residue of limestone rocks. The best agricultural soil in Greece is located along the coast and consists of

A climber scales the slopes of Mount Olympus.

Geography of Greece

Map labels:

Skopje
Tirane
MACEDONIA
BULGARIA
TURKEY
ALBANIA
Lake Prespa
Strymon
Kavalla
Komotiní
Alexandroupolis
Sea of Marmara
Axios
Lake Kastoria
Thessaloníki
Haliacmon
Kozáni
Mount Olympus
Mount Athos
Ioánnina
Lárissa
Gulf of Thermai
Aegean Sea
Limnos
Corfu
Corfu
Lake Ioánnina
Pindus Mountains
Volos
Sporades
Mytilene
Lesbos
TURKEY
Lamía
Delphi
Mount Parnassus
Euboea
Khalkis
Chios
Cephalonia
Gulf of Patras
Gulf of Corinth
Patras
Attica
Andros
Samos
Corinth
Piraeus
Athens
Vári
Saronic Gulf
Hermoúpolis
Peloponnesus
Trípolis
Sparta
Ionian Sea
Cyclades
Rhodes
Cape Matapan
Cythera
Dodecanese Islands
Rhodes
Sea of Crete
Khania
Crete
Iráklion
Mediterranean Sea

Legend:

- Cropland
- Pasture
- Forest
- Mountain region

- - - International boundary
⊛ National capital
• City or village

0   50 Miles
0   50 Kilometers

NORTH ↑

Geography of Greece

loam and clay. In contrast with the dry soil of the mountain regions, the coastal soil sometimes needs to be drained before it can be used for farming.

Historians theorize that in ancient times Greece probably had many forests, but that these were depleted over time for their wood. Forests are still threatened by development, wildfires, and clearing for grazing. Still, approximately one-fifth of the country is currently forested; much of this land is protected by government regulations.

THE CORINTH CANAL

The Corinth Canal links the Aegean and Ionian Seas through the Isthmus of Corinth at the northernmost point of the Peloponnese. It was opened in 1893 and was meant to save small sailing ships from the more dangerous sea route around Cape Matapan. Today the canal is too narrow for many modern ships and is used mostly for tourist boats. The road bridge above the canal has become a very popular place for bungee jumping. Jumpers leap 148 feet (45 m) down from a staging platform beneath the bridge.

Greece is also a land of rivers, but they are generally small. Few can be used for transportation because they are shallow, with turbulent currents that make boat travel difficult. The longest rivers include the Haliacmon, the Axios, and the Strymon. The Evros River forms the border between Greece and Turkey. Rivers are used for recreational activities, and the areas around them are often protected. Greece also

AVERAGE TEMPERATURE AND PRECIPITATION

Region (City)	Average January Temperature Minimum/Maximum	Average July Temperature Minimum/Maximum	Average Precipitation January/July
Southern coastal (Athens)	44/55°F (7/13°C)	73/89°F (23/27°C)	1.9/0.2 inches (4.8/0.51 cm)
Northern mainland (Thessaloníki)	34/48°F (1/9°C)	66/88°F (19/31°C)	1.6/0.9 inches (4.8/2.2 cm)
Crete (Iráklion)	48/58°F (8/14°C)	72/83°F (22/28°C)	3.7/0 inches (9/0 cm)[7]

has dozens of lakes. Among the largest are Kastoria, Ioánnina, and Prespa. Many of the lakes, lagoons, and wetlands are also protected areas.

CLIMATE AND WEATHER

Because of its Mediterranean location, Greece's climate is generally mild. However, it varies depending on the region. The mountains in Western Greece and the Peloponnesian region can get heavy, wet snow in the

Small fishing villages ring the shores of Lake Prespa.

Legend:
- Arid Steppe, Hot
- Arid Steppe, Cold
- Temperate, Dry and Hot Summer
- Temperate, Dry and Warm Summer
- Temperate, No Dry Season, Hot Summer
- Temperate, No Dry Season, Warm Summer
- Cold, Dry and Warm Summer
- Cold, No Dry Season, Warm Summer
- Cold, No Dry Season, Cold Summer

Climate of Greece

winter, plenty of rain in the spring and fall, and hot days during the summer. The coast along the Ionian Sea has milder temperatures, but it gets more rain than any other region. In Macedonia and Thrace, the rainfall is spread more evenly throughout the year and temperatures are also milder. Athens is hot in the summer. It holds the record for the hottest temperature ever recorded in Europe—118.4 degrees Fahrenheit (48°C).[8] The city almost never sees temperatures below freezing in the winter, although it receives most of its rain at that time.

The lowest temperature ever recorded in Athens was 25°F (-4°C).

CHAPTER 3

ANIMALS AND NATURE: ENVIRONMENT AT RISK

Greece's varied topography, ranging from islands to peninsulas to rugged mountains, has resulted in a wide assortment of animals in the nation's land, skies, and seas. The national animal is the dolphin, suggesting the country's link to the seas that surround it. There was even a minor Greek dolphin god named Delphinus, a servant of the sea god Poseidon. However, the habitats of Greece's dolphin populations are being threatened by changes in the ecosystem. Environmental groups are working to protect these iconic mammals.

Orcas, the largest dolphins, can grow to 30 feet (9.5 m) in length.

Greece has many other kinds of animals that live in or near the sea. These include loggerhead turtles, shrimp, mussels, crabs, octopuses, and more than 200 identified varieties of fish. Fishing

Dolphins are Greece's national animals. They feature in several Greek myths.

SEA SPONGE DIVING

Diving for natural sea sponges was once the livelihood of many Greeks who lived in coastal areas. However, the invention of synthetic sponges, along with an epidemic that infected most of the sponges in the Mediterranean in 1986, caused a decline in the sponge diving industry. One of the few places left where sponge diving still takes place is on the island of Kalymnos. Before the epidemic, Kalymnos was rich in sponges due to its warm water temperatures. In the old days, sponge divers would locate a sponge bed and then dive down to it, using a flat stone called a *skandalopetra* to reach the bottom more quickly. Then the diver would cut the sponges free and put them into a special net to take them to the surface. How deep the diver would go, and how long he could stay submerged, depended on his lung capacity. Today sponge divers often use compressed air to breathe when they dive.

is one of the country's top industries. Sea sponges, simple multicelled animals that live on the sea floor, can be found in the waters of Greece. Diving for sponges to harvest and sell is a Greek tradition. Other animals that live in Greek seas include swordfish, squid, and the Mediterranean monk seal, which is an endangered species. The coast is also home to pelicans, storks, and egrets.

Greece's mountain regions and forests feature a variety of bigger mammals. Wild boars, brown bears, red deer, golden jackals, and a few wolves can be found in forested areas. In the mountains, chamois and ibex (two kinds of mountain goats) can be found, and a rare species of white goat lives on the island of Crete. Lynxes, foxes, badgers, and

Sea sponges for sale in a Greek market

weasels are also common. Endangered species in Greece include several species of mice, bats, and shrews.

A WALK IN THE WOODS

Greece's forests are made up of a wide variety of trees. White poplar, spearheaded cypress, chestnut, pine, and fir trees grow in Greece. Olive trees, which are grown in groves throughout the country, can live for hundreds of years. Their fruit is eaten or pressed into olive oil. Orange, date, pomegranate, and fig trees are also cultivated in Greece.

One of Greece's most unusual trees grows on the island of Chios in the eastern Aegean Sea. Mastic trees produce a rare resin that is collected and sold, providing the island's most

OLIVE TREES

The olive tree and the oil made from its fruit have always been very important to Greek culture. Greece was one of the first places where olive trees were cultivated. Before, they simply grew wild all over the Mediterranean. An olive tree can live from 300 to 600 years, and there are an estimated 120 million olive trees in Greece. The country is the third-largest producer of olive oil and one of the biggest consumers of it.[1] Cretans consume more olive oil than other Greeks. Their diet is said to be among the healthiest in the world.

Greece is known for its olive trees.

important export. The resin, also called mastic, is harvested by cutting incisions into the trees' bark so that the resin will flow out in tear-shaped droplets. Mastic is used to make chewing gum, spices, alcoholic beverages, and candy. The EU has declared that only mastic produced on Chios can legally be sold as genuine mastic. Mastic has been such an important part of Chios throughout history that some of the island's fortresses were built to protect its mastic trees.

Greece is also known for its beautiful wildflowers. Many of these flowers are familiar to anyone who has read Greek mythology: anemones, laurel, hyacinths, violets, tulips, primrose, chamomile, peonies, narcissus, and parthenium.

UNDER THREAT

The lush, majestic environment of modern Greece is threatened by air and water pollution. In the 1970s, Greece rapidly

SAVING GREEK ANIMALS

The British organization Saving Greek Animals is dedicated to improving the lives of animals in Greece. While Greece has animal protection legislation, these laws are not always enforced. Greece does not have a large animal welfare organization like the American Society for the Prevention of Cruelty to Animals, and smaller organizations are often underfunded. Saving Greek Animals assists with spaying and neutering animals, rescuing abandoned or unwanted donkeys, and providing veterinary surgical supplies and medicine.

Mastic drips from a tree in its characteristic teardrop shape.

industrialized, resulting in heavy air pollution from factories. The problem was compounded with exhaust from diesel-powered vehicles. In Athens, air pollution has been so severe that the government has frequently declared air quality emergencies. Air pollution is bad not only for people, causing respiratory ailments, but also for Athens's ancient monuments. Acid rain and particles in the air erode marble structures, slowly destroying Greece's architectural heritage. The government has attempted to put controls in place to combat air pollution, including emission restrictions on vehicles, but it remains a problem.

Water pollution is another issue facing Greece, resulting from the discharge of industrial runoff, sewage, and municipal wastewater into

COASTAL "DEAD ZONES"

In 2006, environmental agencies from the United Nations and the EU reported the devastating effect that water pollution has on Greece's coastal waters. In Athens, runoff from approximately 1,000 nearby industrial plants resulted in severe pollution in the Bay of Elefsis. At the same time, the city's sewage system was found insufficient to prevent further pollutants from entering the water. One official from the environmental group Greenpeace said, "Some areas in the bays of Athens and Thessaloníki are complete dead zones. For some, there is no chance of ever recovering."[2]

Industrialization has resulted in severe air pollution in many urban areas of Greece.

ENDANGERED SPECIES IN GREECE

According to the International Union for Conservation of Nature (IUCN), Greece is home to the following number of species that are categorized by the organization as Critically Endangered, Endangered, or Vulnerable:

Mammals	10
Birds	10
Reptiles	8
Amphibians	5
Fishes	75
Mollusks	63
Other Invertebrates	27
Plants	55
Total	253[3]

the sea. The problem is particularly acute in the bays of Athens and Thessaloníki.

Greece has signed several environmental treaties, including the Kyoto Protocol, which calls for limits to greenhouse gas emissions that may be contributing to global warming. It has also signed treaties concerning pollution and marine conservation. In 2010, Greece was the twenty-first country to ratify a global water treaty that aimed to reduce conflicts over waterways that form or cross international boundaries.

Greece must also defend against natural environmental threats such as forest fires.

NATIONAL PARKS

Park Name	Region
Prespa Lakes	Western Macedonia
Mount Olympus	Central Macedonia
Vikos-Aoos	Epirus
Pindus	Epirus
Alonissos Island	Thessaly
Mount Parnassus	Central Greece
Mount Oeta	Central Greece
Mount Parnitha	Attica
Sounio	Attica
Ainos	Ionian Islands
Zakynthos	Ionian Islands
Samaria Gorge	Crete

GREECE'S PROTECTED AREAS

One of Greece's greatest conservation successes is its national parks system. Greece's 12 national parks are protected areas where the plants,

The National Marine Park of Alonissos

animals, and geography are of particular interest. The particular species and landscapes protected vary by region. Mount Olympus features more than 1,700 species of plants.[4] Pindus National Park features several

rare bird species. At the National Marine Park of Zakynthos, the Sea Turtle Protection Society of Greece works to protect loggerhead sea turtles and their nesting habitat.

In addition to national parks, Greece recognizes aesthetic forests (areas that are especially beautiful or important to tourism), protected monuments of nature, and game and hunting reserves, all of which are protected to some degree.

PRESPA LAKES NATIONAL PARK

Prespa Lakes consists of two lakes, Megali and Mikri, or the Big and the Small Lake. It is the only national park in Greece that consists mostly of water. Greece shares the lakes with the countries of Macedonia and Albania. The lakes are estimated to be more than 5 million years old. They are home to hundreds of species of plants, dozens of different species of mammals, and many species of birds. These include the Dalmatian pelican, considered by experts to be a vulnerable species.

CHAPTER 4

HISTORY: LAND OF THE ANCIENTS

People have lived in the caves and on the hilltops of Greece since prehistoric times, but one of the first major cultures to flourish was the Minoan civilization, dating back to approximately 3000 BCE. The civilization's name for itself has been lost to history, so archaeologists named it after King Minos, a legendary Greek king mentioned in Homer's *Odyssey*. The Minoans lived on the island of Crete. They traded with other people in the Mediterranean, and they were among the first Europeans to develop a system of writing. By 1580 BCE, the Minoans had spread to several other Greek islands, expanding their farming and trading operations. They left behind not just small artifacts such as pottery, but also the ruins of entire palaces decorated with spectacular frescoes.

The ruins of a Minoan palace in Crete

At about the same time, another civilization was established in Greece when invaders from the north swept in and conquered many settlements. These new people built walled, fortified cities, and spread to other Greek islands and into Asia Minor (modern-day western Turkey). They had established settlements on the mainland by 1650 BCE. The biggest city was Mycenae, so they are known as the Mycenaeans. The myths and legends of the Mycenaeans are thought to be the basis for later Greek myths.

Around 1600 BCE, the volcano that forms the island of Santorini erupted and destroyed many cities. The massive explosion crippled the surrounding area and likely led to the decline of the Minoan civilization. In approximately 1150 BCE, Greek invaders from the north overran them. The city of Mycenae continued to exist as a weakened city-state until the second century CE, but its civilization vanished as well. As the Minoan and Mycenaean civilizations dwindled, arts, culture, and trade faded and Greek

THE CYCLOPEAN WALLS

Among the most amazing archaeological structures left by the Mycenaeans are the Cyclopean Walls. These fortifications are constructed from huge, largely unchiseled boulders with almost no gaps between them and no mortar. Building the walls required a careful selection of boulders that would fit together without being altered. The walls were so big that Greeks of the Classical era thought only giants such as the mythical Cyclops could have built them.

settlements became isolated. This period is sometimes called Greece's Dark Age.

BACK INTO THE LIGHT

Eventually, Greek civilization emerged from its dark era. During the archaic period, from approximately 700 to 480 BCE, city-states such as Athens, Sparta, Corinth, and Thebes thrived. Many different classes of people—including citizens, foreigners, and slaves—lived together in these city-states. It took a great deal of political organization to run a large city-state smoothly. In Athens in the fifth century BCE, this led to one of the earliest instances of democracy, which differed significantly from what we know today: only free Athenian males over the age of 18 were allowed to vote. Any male citizen who wanted to participate could attend meetings of the Assembly, held forty times per year. Votes were conducted by a show of hands. Soon the concept of city-states spread to neighboring lands as well, and a trading network was reestablished in the Mediterranean.

Athens is one of the world's oldest cities.

The Archaic period was followed by the classical period, when Athens and Sparta dominated Greece with their military and cultural achievements. The rise of Athens was aided by favorable geography, including natural mountain defenses, water supplies, and a long coastline. Athenians emphasized philosophy and art—a stark contrast to Sparta, which downplayed these in favor of military might. Spartans

The School of Athens, **a fresco by the famous Italian artist Raphael, depicts Plato and Aristotle at its center.**

also dismissed the democracy of Athens. They were ruled instead by kings while at war and by a 30-member Senate in peacetime. The two city-states joined forces to defeat the Persians in 480 BCE. The victory

led to what has been called the Golden Age of Athens. The names of those who lived and worked in fifth-century BCE Athens are immortal. Playwrights such as Aeschylus, Sophocles, Euripides, and Aristophanes, the philosophers Plato and Socrates, the historian Thucydides, and the orator Demosthenes all called the city their home. Most of the major temples on the Acropolis were built during this time, including the Parthenon.

Less than 50 years into this period, Athens and Sparta turned on each other, each leading its own alliance of city-states in the Peloponnesian War (431–404 BCE). Pericles, the leader who

GREEK PHILOSOPHERS

The greatest philosophers of ancient Greece were Socrates, Plato, and Aristotle. It was through Socrates that the term *philosopher* came into wide usage. He sought to educate people indirectly, asking them questions that would lead them to reconsider errors in their own thinking. Socrates was eventually condemned to death on charges of corrupting the youth of Athens.

Plato was one of Socrates's students. He wrote on many topics, including the nature of knowledge and the ideal state. Plato was extremely influential; the English mathematician and philosopher Alfred North Whitehead later quipped "the safest general characterization of the European philosophical tradition is that it consists of a series of footnotes to Plato."[1]

Aristotle was a student of Plato and the tutor of Alexander the Great. After Alexander became king, Aristotle returned to Athens to start a school. He went on to make major contributions to the study of logic.

had shepherded Athens through its Golden Age and ordered the construction of the Parthenon, led the Athenians. But his singular focus on naval power and his strategy of abandoning territory to the Spartans without a fight prevented any major Athenian gains. Following more than two decades of war, the Spartan general Lysander finally forced Athens to surrender in 404 BCE. The victory resulted in Spartan control over all of Greece, but several subsequent wars weakened Sparta. In 338 BCE Philip II of Macedon, invading from the northeast, effectively conquered the Greek mainland with the assistance of his son Alexander.

Alexander the Great went on to lead military campaigns against Persia and into Asia. He expanded the influence of Greek culture far beyond the traditional city-states. However, after Alexander's early death at age 32, much of his empire fell apart. As the Roman culture grew in Italy and the West, Romans invaded Greece and began ruling it in the second and first century BCE. The Roman conquerors adopted much from the culture of the Greeks. Roman rule brought a period of peace to Greece until the Roman Empire split in the fourth century CE. The eastern part, including Greece, became known as the Byzantine Empire.

BYZANTINE GREECE

Though Greece enjoyed stability and prosperity under the Byzantine Empire, it was not insulated from the political, military, economic, and religious challenges that befell the empire during its millennium-long existence. Byzantine scholars preserved ancient Greek and Latin texts, and artists and architects developed styles that would influence the

MAXIMIANVS

culture of the Eastern Mediterranean for years to come. However, as the Byzantine emperor Justinian expanded his territory into Africa, Italy, and Spain during the sixth century, he drained the empire's coffers and

also left Greece without military protection. The Byzantine Empire was under constant attack, and Greece was not spared. Groups from Europe, including the Ostrogoths, invaded Greece and established their own territories there. The Byzantines began recapturing these regions around the end of the eighth century, though some more remote areas were not retaken for hundreds of years.

As a result of the Fourth Crusade in 1204, Greece fell under the control of the Franks, who came from Western Europe. The conquests were short lived, however. By the end of the thirteenth century, the Byzantines had once again captured the central and southern portions of Greece. Byzantine rule ended when the Ottoman Turks captured the Byzantine capital Constantinople (modern-day Istanbul) in 1453.

REDISCOVERING CLASSICAL GREECE

During the late eighteenth and early nineteenth centuries, Greek intellectuals revived interest in the study of the ancient Greeks. Those who traveled to Western Europe to study at universities encountered Enlightenment principles. Especially stirring to them was the fact that ancient Greece was held in high regard by the intellectuals with whom the Greeks studied. Books written for Greeks about ancient Greece became popular, though mostly among the well-off and upper class people who had already left Ottoman-controlled Greece. Some of the authors of these books tried to ignite an uprising against both the Ottomans and the Orthodox Church by popularizing the wonders of classical Greece. However, interest in these ideas did not extend to the poorer classes of Greece, and the intellectual movement alone would not lead to the overthrow of the Turks.

The Turks controlled Greece's cities, ports, and islands, and the Turkish sultans who ruled the country used Greece as a source of wealth and soldiers. Greece was cut off from the scientific and economic growth of the rest of Europe, and little development occurred for almost four hundred years. The Turks permitted the continued existence of the Greek Orthodox Church, but Christians were treated as second-class citizens by their Muslim rulers. By the late eighteenth century, the Greeks had begun rebuilding their economy, and organized resistance movements began to form. Occasional armed revolts took place, but were always put down by the Turks.

Finally, the Greeks launched the Greek War of Independence (1821–1832). The United Kingdom, France, and Russia came to the aid of the Greeks. These countries wanted to preserve their trading ties to Greece and reduce Turkey's power in the Mediterranean, so they pledged to help Greece win its independence. Greece was victorious, declaring its independence in 1830. Despite its military victories over the Ottoman Empire, the newborn nation of Greece continued to be afflicted by political and economic instability. In 1833, Greece's new allies stepped in again and installed King Otto on the Greek throne. Otto proved unpopular, however, and he was overthrown in 1862. King George I came to power in 1863. George would go on to reign for nearly 50 years.

King Otto was only 17 years old when his reign began.

INDEPENDENCE

Once Greece had established itself as an independent nation, it set out to regain all Greek-speaking territories. During the second half of the nineteenth century and the first part of the twentieth century, Greece annexed neighboring islands and territories that had Greek-speaking populations. With help from some of the Balkan countries, the Turks were driven out of Macedonia during the First Balkan War (1912–1913). When the members of the alliance rushed to claim the reconquered territory, they came into conflict amongst themselves. The Second Balkan War (1913) began when Bulgaria attacked its former allies Greece and Serbia. Bulgaria was defeated, and Greece added southern Macedonia and Crete to its territory.

At the beginning of World War I (1914–1918), Greece remained neutral, joining neither the Allied Powers, which included France and the United Kingdom, nor the Central Powers, which included Germany and Bulgaria. Despite efforts by the Allied Powers to recruit the Greeks, the country maintained its neutrality during the early years of the war. Finally, in June 1917, Greece declared war on the Central Powers. Greek troops fought alongside French and British soldiers. The Allied victory in 1918 allowed Greece to acquire Western Thrace from Bulgaria.

The Communist Party of Greece was founded in 1918.

Following the war, in 1923, revolutionaries attempted to unseat the king and bring about an elected

government. They were initially successful, but the minister of war declared himself prime minister in 1925. He then proclaimed himself dictator in 1926. He was deposed only a few months later, and a period of relative stability followed until 1935. In that year, a military coup reinstated the monarchy.

The 1920s and 1930s were marked by internal political instability and power struggles, but the most significant shock to Greek society was the Asia Minor Disaster. After a failed Greek attempt to recapture Greek cities on the west coast of Turkey, the Turks drove the Greek populations out of Asia Minor in 1922. In the midst of the mayhem, many Greeks, Armenians, and Jews were killed or forced to flee their ancestral homes. Greece took in thousands of refugees, many of whom had lost all their possessions. It took the country many years to absorb this huge influx of immigrants and to provide the necessary infrastructure, schooling, and job opportunities.

By 1936, Greece's monarchy had again grown strong, and a new dictator

RELATIONS WITH TURKEY

Greece and Turkey have had an uneasy relationship. Older Greeks still remember the atrocities that took place when Turkey drove out the Greek populations from Asia Minor. However, while the Greeks might fear the Turkish government, they do not fear the average Turkish people themselves. In 1999, when terrible earthquakes struck both countries, their citizens were quick to help each other recover. Greece later supported Turkish membership in the EU. People from Greece make up one of the largest groups of tourists in Turkey.

by the name of Ioannis Metaxas showed some alarming fascist leanings. However, Metaxas died in January 1941, just a few months before the nation was thrust into World War II (1939–1945).

Greece fared much worse during World War II than it had during World War I. The Italian dictator Benito Mussolini unsuccessfully invaded Greece in 1940, but the country was ultimately taken and occupied by Nazi Germany in April 1941. Greece was not liberated until 1944.

Following World War II, the country suffered the Greek Civil War (1946–1949), fought between the government forces and a relatively small Communist army that enjoyed popular support from left-leaning Greeks. The Communists, following the writings of philosopher Karl Marx, sought to establish a society in which all property would be publicly owned, looking to the Communist Soviet Union for direction.

RESISTANCE MOVEMENTS

One of the largest resistance movements in Greece during World War II was the Communist-backed National Liberation Front. This group and its offshoot, the Greek People's Liberation Army, fought the Germans. Female guerilla fighters fought alongside men in the National Liberation Front. After years of political exclusion, the Communists sought a share of the political power after the war.

Nazi troops set up anti-aircraft guns near the Acropolis.

The Greek Communists had fought the German occupation during the war, but they were unwilling to put down their weapons when it became clear the postwar Greek national government wanted to continue to exclude them from power. With British and US support, the Greek national government defeated the Communists in 1949. By 1952, Greece had joined the North Atlantic Treaty Organization (NATO), an alliance of countries pledging mutual defense. Other NATO members include the United States, the United Kingdom, and France.

But things were still not peaceful for Greece. In April 1967, a military junta seized power from the Greek king and parliament. This move revived the persecution of the leftist and Communist forces that had fought the civil war. Greece was ruled by a reactionary military government until 1974, and the king was forced to flee the country. Greek citizens also lost some of their civil rights during this time. Freedom of the press was suspended, political opponents were exiled or imprisoned, and films, music, and books were censored or banned.

The king attempted a counter-coup in December 1967, but it failed within a day.

GREECE ENTERS THE MODERN ERA

Finally, following the military government's collapse in 1974, the Greeks held a referendum that decided the future of the Greek monarchy.

An armored vehicle patrols the streets on December 13, 1967, a few months after the military junta's seizure of the Greek government.

They voted to abolish the monarchy and affirmed democratic rule in Greece. In 1981, Greece joined the EU, and in 2001 it became part of the European Economic and Monetary Union.

Greece was the tenth nation to join the EU.

The global economic crisis beginning in 2007, combined with excessive borrowing by the government, caused Greece's economy to stumble. The problems persisted, and in 2012 the nation held a series of elections in an attempt to create a unified government that could tackle these issues. Today, Greece faces severe economic problems, but a look at its turbulent history shows that the Greek people have experience persevering through difficult crises.

Voters hoped that Antonis Samaras, elected prime minister in June 2012, could begin to solve Greece's economic problems.

CHAPTER 5

PEOPLE: GREEK PRIDE

The majority of the people living in Greece are Greek citizens. Only 7 percent of the population consists of foreigners, though unofficially it may be a few percentage points higher.[1] But the Greek people themselves consist of many ethnic minority groups. These include Turks, Slavs, Albanians, Bulgarians, Armenians, and Vlachs from Serbia. Recent immigrants have come from the Philippines, Poland, Pakistan, China, and African nations. People of the Jewish faith are also considered a minority group, since most of the country adheres to the Greek Orthodox religion. Many of these minority groups are from Turkey, especially near the northern and northeastern borders of Greece. Because of Greece's long history of settlers and invaders from other countries, even people with a long family history of Greek heritage may have other nationalities in their family tree.

Greek families attended a 2011 parade in Thessaloníki.

YOU SAY IT!

English	Greek
Hello	Yassou (YAH-soo)
Goodbye	Kherete (KHEHR-eh-tay)
How are you?	Ti kanis? (tee KAH-nihs)
Sorry	Signomi (seeg-NOH-mee)
Thank you	Efkharisto (ehff-kah-rees-TOH)
You're welcome	Parakalo (pah-rah-kah-LOH)

LANGUAGE

Most of the people in Greece speak Greek as their primary language. The exceptions are those people who belong to one of the Turkish minority

A Serbian immigrant plays the accordion on an Athens street.

groups and speak Turkish as their first language. Most of these people live in Thrace or on the Dodecanese Islands. Along the northern borders with the Balkan countries, some Greek citizens speak Slavic languages such as Bulgarian or Macedonian. Approximately 1 percent of the country also speaks English or French natively.[2]

The modern Greek language derives from the language spoken in ancient times. Greek is one of the world's oldest known written languages. Examples of Greek writing have been found on clay tablets dating to the fifteenth century BCE, although the classical Greek alphabet was not invented until centuries later. Spoken Greek, which is called demotic Greek, has evolved to include elements from other languages. Words and phrases have come from Turkish, Albanian, Italian, French, and English. Ancient Greek is different enough from modern Greek that today's Greeks have to study ancient Greek in order to read it fluently.

Greek has approximately 12 million speakers worldwide.

Two other special forms of Greek, *koine* and *katharevousa*, were used for specific purposes. Koine is the language of the original New Testament of the Bible, and it has been used by the clergy of the Greek Orthodox Church. Katharevousa was invented in the nineteenth century in an effort to remove foreign loanwords from the language. The word *katharevousa* is related to an ancient Greek word meaning "pure," and proponents hoped it would become a purified form of the modern Greek

An ancient Greek inscription found on ruins in Turkey

language, easier to learn than classical Greek. During the nineteenth and twentieth centuries, there was an ongoing struggle over whether katharevousa or demotic Greek would become the official language. The unpopular military dictatorship of 1967–1974 heavily favored katharevousa. When the regime fell, so did the language. Katharevousa ceased to be the official language of Greece in 1976, and demotic Greek took over. Katharevousa is now basically obsolete and is rarely used.

The Greek alphabet has 24 letters. It was the basis for other alphabets, including the Latin and Cyrillic alphabets. It was also the first to use vowels. Even the word *alphabet* comes from the Greek language, since it uses the first two letters of the Greek alphabet, *alpha* and *beta*.

Greek is also the official language of the island of Cyprus.

LIVING IN GREECE

More than 60 percent of Greece's population lives in urban areas, and most of the rural areas are sparsely populated. Historically, many Greeks lived in small villages, cut off from other people, and as a result they forged very close family relationships, which continue today. In 2011, the birthrate in Greece was 9.08 births per 1,000 people, or approximately 0.16 percent.[3] Greece's birthrate ranks among the lowest of any country's.

Greece's rural areas are much less densely populated than its urban areas.

LOW BIRTHRATES

The birthrate in Greece is extremely low. In 2011, only 9.08 babies were born for every 1,000 people who live in Greece. In comparison, the birthrate in the United States is 13.68 births per 1,000 people.[4] Some economists link this phenomenon to the cost of living, the country's economic problems, and the fact that Greeks who want a better standard of living may only have one child or none at all. Others feel it is a result of an increasing divorce rate among Greek couples.

Greek gender roles have undergone dramatic change in recent decades. Traditionally, the men worked while women stayed at home and raised the children. Today, improved school and childcare access means that women in Greece have greater freedom to work if they so choose. Greek women received the right to vote in 1952, and laws establishing gender equality in work and family relationships were passed in 1983. Men and women share much more legal equality in Greece than they once did.

Throughout the twentieth century, many Greeks left their home country for Western Europe, Canada, Australia, and the United States, looking for better opportunities. This group of Greeks who no longer live in their country is referred to as the diaspora, or the dispersion of people from their original homeland.

Population Density of Greece

The median age in Greece is 42.5 years, and the average person lives to approximately 80.[5] While Greece has been rated as having some of the most affordable healthcare in the European Union, its economic problems and widespread unemployment have made it hard for many Greeks to navigate the healthcare system and to afford the additional costs sometimes required to ensure adequate care. Doctors at public hospitals often have long waiting lists, and there is also a shortage of hospitals outside of urban areas.

More than 90 percent of people in Greece

MOUNT ATHOS

Mount Athos (or Agion Oros, which means "holy mountain" in Greek) is located on a peninsula in northern Greece and is the home of 20 Greek Orthodox monasteries. The largest monastery, the Great Lavra, was founded in 963 CE. The region of Mount Athos is inhabited only by monks. Outsider men can receive permission to visit the peninsula, but women, boys, and even most female animals are not allowed at all. Though each monastery is self-governed, an administrator appointed by the Greek government supervises the community. Currently there are more than 1,000 monks living on Mount Athos. In addition to the large monasteries, there are 12 smaller communities, as well as numerous dwellings for solitary monks. The population of the monks has risen and fallen through history as various groups have controlled Greece and affected the wealth and independence of the monasteries.

The 20 Greek Orthodox monasteries on Mount Athos can only be visited by men.

DODEKATHEISTS

One of the smaller, non-mainstream religious movements in Greece is that of the Dodekatheists. They do not form a recognized religion and have no set beliefs or formal memberships. The group rejects monotheistic religions and instead seeks to return to the polytheism of the ancient Greeks, who worshipped many different gods and goddesses.

religiously identify as Greek Orthodox.[6] The remaining people are largely Muslim, Roman Catholic, Protestant, or atheist. Greece once had a large population of Jewish people, but this changed during World War II. Greek Jews suffered harshly at the hands of the Nazis. Most were killed during forced deportations or in Nazi concentration camps. The Greek Orthodox Christian religion originated in Eastern Orthodoxy, which was practiced and spread by the Byzantine Empire.

The government supports the Greek Orthodox religion, which is taught in schools. Religion plays an important but perhaps dwindling role in the lives of many Greeks, who tend to observe the most important religious holidays, including Christmas and especially Easter. Greece is divided into 81 dioceses, or religious districts; a bishop of the church controls each diocese. Other groups of bishops deal with the church's day-to-day business and decision-making.

Prime Minister Antonis Samaras meets with a Greek Orthodox official in 2012.

CHAPTER 6

CULTURE: HOME OF THE OLYMPICS

Many of the cultural legacies of Greece have made their way around the world, from foods to literature to architecture. But probably the best-known of all Greek traditions is the Olympic Games. Historians believe the first Olympic Games took place in 776 BCE. Until the fourth century CE, they took place every four years on the plains of Olympia (in the Peloponnese region), and were dedicated to the gods. At first they were a one-day event, but were later expanded to three days, then five. Events included running races, the long jump, the pentathlon, boxing, equestrian events, and a type of martial arts called *pankration*. However, in 393 CE, Emperor Theodosius I declared all pagan events should be banned. The Olympics stopped and were not reborn until 1896.

Winners in the ancient Olympics did not receive money but were often treated as celebrities.

Panathenaic Stadium was the site of the first modern Olympic Games. It was reconstructed from the ruins of an ancient Greek stadium.

THE MODERN OLYMPICS

The first modern Olympics were held in Athens in April 1896. Following some Greek initiatives, a young Frenchman named Pierre de Coubertin proposed bringing back the games as an international competition. The International Olympic Committee (IOC) was formed, and since then the games have taken place every four years, except for several years during the World Wars. In 2004, the Summer Olympic Games once again took place in Athens. The tradition of carrying a torch lit in Olympia to the site of the games began in 1936 and continues today.

However, there is more to Greek sports than the Olympics. Soccer is the biggest sport, as it is in many countries across Europe. Other favored sports include tennis, golf, ice hockey, cycling, and basketball. Greece's vast coastlines have also made water sports popular.

MADE IN GREECE

Much of the modern artwork found in Greece has been inspired by the Greek art of antiquity. Mosaics, terra cotta pottery, bronze statues, marble sculptures, and painted religious icons are all popular. Leather sandals, pottery, and replicas of ancient Greek art are all sold to visitors in local markets. There are also many excellent contemporary Greek artists who paint landscapes, portraits, and abstract motifs.

Pottery is sold at open-air markets across the country, including this one in Crete.

Greece is also known for its music. Music was an important part of theater and literature in ancient Greece, and it was closely intertwined with dancing and poetry. During the Byzantine era, music was mostly related to church services and was heavily influenced by Eastern musical traditions. Many Greek folk songs date back to the Byzantine and Ottoman eras or even earlier. Owing to Greece's geographic location and history, today's Greek music is still influenced by the neighboring cultures of Western Europe, the Balkans, and the Middle East. Instruments, styles, and melodies from across these regions are filtered through the Greek experience to create a uniquely Greek sound. Traditional Greek music is usually accompanied by instruments such as bagpipes, flutes, tambourines, drums, violins, and the bouzouki, a stringed instrument like a lute or guitar. The second half of the twentieth century saw an important, independent movement of Greek composers who set contemporary

HOMEGROWN MUSIC

The musical landscape of Greece has avoided being overshadowed by the pop music from the United States and the United Kingdom that finds its way onto music charts around the world. Greek artists generally outnumber those from elsewhere on the Greek charts, even in modern genres such as hip-hop.

A musician plays a bouzouki. The instrument has its origins in ancient Greek instruments.

Greek poetry to music and created the popular art song genre. This form gained political significance in the late 1960s and 1970s.

Greek dance is also an important part of the culture. In ancient times, dance was one of the highest forms of the performing arts. The ancient Greeks danced to prepare for war, to accompany plays, and to express emotions. Today most traditional Greek dances are in a form known as *syrtos*. The performers dance in a circle, linked to each other either by a folded handkerchief or by holding each other's hands, wrists, or shoulders. The dance starts with the right foot and moves counter-clockwise, usually in a shuffling motion. There is also a livelier and more energetic form of dance in which dancers leap and spring into the air.

There are thousands of traditional dances from Greece's various regions.

WORDS, ANCIENT AND MODERN

The most famous Greek literature is thousands of years old. Many of the epic poems, dramas, and philosophical dialogues written by ancient Greeks such as Homer, Plato, Aristotle, Herodotus, and Aeschylus are still read and studied today. Many students still study the ancient epics, the *Iliad* and the *Odyssey*. Modern Greek literature includes a category

A second-century CE bust of Homer. No images exist from during Homer's lifetime, around the eighth century BCE, so the image is an idealized one.

known as the New Athenian School, whose writers were inspired by Greek folklore to keep traditional Greek forms of storytelling and poetry alive.

Following World War II, many writers wrote about their experiences during the conflict. Nikos Kazantzakis, author of the novel *Zorba the Greek*, is one of the best-known modern Greek writers. One of his most famous poems was a retelling of the ancient Greek story of Odysseus in modern language. In 1963, poet Giorgos Seferis was awarded the Nobel Prize in Literature for his poems and essays. Writer Odysseas Elytis received a Nobel Prize in Literature in 1979 for his poetry.

GREEK ARCHITECTURE

The remains of ancient temples, theaters, and other buildings can still be found throughout Greece today. These durable monuments to Greece's history owe their longevity to the materials used to build them: marble and limestone. The engineers and architects who designed the buildings even developed impressive forms of earthquake-proof construction, using iron clamps in lead casings to allow some flexibility in the structures.

The Greeks developed three different styles of construction, called orders: Doric, Ionic, and Corinthian. Doric, the simplest order, can be seen in the construction of the Parthenon. Ionic, a more delicate order,

The Corinthian order is the most detailed of the ancient Greek styles.

is visible at the temple to Athena Nike. Finally, Corinthian, the most elaborate and ornate order, was the least common type used by the Greeks. Elements of classical architecture are found in many buildings around the world, including the US Capitol Building and the Lincoln Memorial, which was constructed to look like the Parthenon in Athens.

RETSINA AND OUZO

Two of Greece's traditional alcoholic beverages are retsina and ouzo. Retsina is a type of white wine flavored with pine resin. It has a very strong pine flavor. It is said the combination comes from the days of sailing ships, when wine had to have other ingredients to keep it from spoiling. Pine resin, which was always present on board ships for use as caulking, was one of these ingredients. Ouzo is an alcoholic liquor that has an anise or licorice taste. It is very strong, and it is often drunk with salty snacks or with seafood.

GREEK FOODS

Art, music, and architecture are not the only contributions Greek culture has made to the world. Many of the traditional foods of Greece have become international favorites. A staple of Greek cuisine is the olive, eaten raw after curing or pressed into olive oil and used in cooking. Greeks also enjoy a wide variety of salads. Bread is a part of every meal, whether bought fresh

A waiter serves a lobster dish at a restaurant in Crete. Seafood is popular in Greece, owing to the strong fishing industry.

from a bakery or made at home. Pita, flat bread made without yeast, is used to roll up other foods. Hard, dried bread pieces known as *paximadia* are dipped in hot milk or coffee at breakfast or used as a bed on which to serve salads with olive oil dressing. *Koulouria*, round pieces of bread that look like bagels, are eaten as snacks and sold by street vendors.

Greek gyro sandwiches have become popular in the United States.

Other famous Greek dishes include *souvlaki*, grilled meat on a skewer, moussaka, baked eggplant lasagna with cheese sauce, and spanakopita, spinach pie. Popular desserts include baklava, made with layers of dough, honey, and nuts, and *loukoumia*, which is similar to gummi bear candy but square and dusted with sugar.

The Greek diet once emphasized home cooking. Like other healthy Mediterranean diets, it included fresh fruits and vegetables, some dairy in the form of cheese and yogurt, limited egg consumption, some poultry and fish, limited red meat, and olive oil instead of butter or lard. However, as the pace of modern life has become more hectic, many Greeks are no longer eating this traditional diet and are instead relying on processed foods.

CELEBRATING THE HOLIDAYS

Many Greek foods are tied to specific holidays and festivals throughout the year. Most festivals are linked to the Greek Orthodox religion.

Christmas and Easter are the two most important holidays on the Greek calendar. Although Christmas is celebrated on December 25, gifts are not exchanged until New Year's Day. In one New Year's tradition, the youngest child in the house throws a pomegranate on the doorstep hard enough to break it open, and then reenters the house with the right foot first to bring good luck to the household. Traditional Christmas foods include *christopsomo*, a slightly sweet bread, *melomakarona*, a cookie covered with honey syrup and walnuts, and *kourabiedes*, a shortbread cookie made with almonds and covered with white powdered sugar.

Easter is the most important Greek religious holiday. Traditional foods are prepared, such as *tsoureki*, a slightly sweet bread with an Easter egg nestled into it. Greek Easter eggs are traditionally red, symbolizing the blood and rebirth of Jesus. A favorite Easter game is *tsougrisma*,

SAINT'S DAYS

A Greek who has the same first name as a saint will celebrate that saint's feast day as if it was his or her own birthday. The household of the person whose name day it is will receive visitors and offer them food and drinks such as coffee and cakes. Only children receive gifts on their name day. If a Greek does not have a saint's name, then he or she celebrates on All Saint's Day.

There are special greetings for Saint's Days. On a person's Saint Day or birthday, one might say "many happy returns" or "many years."

in which two people each hold an Easter egg and hit them together. The one whose egg cracks first loses.

Not all Greek holidays are religious. Greek Independence Day is celebrated on March 25, commemorating the first day of the Greek War of Independence, and Labor Day is celebrated on May 1. The holiday of Polytechneio Day is observed on November 17 in remembrance of the 1973 student protests against the right-wing military dictatorship.

Authorities killed more than 20 people during the 1973 student protests.

Greek sporting events, architecture, literature, and cuisine have influenced the western world for thousands of years. But one of Greece's greatest legacies endures in the field of government: the system of democracy.

Tsoureki **and other traditional Easter breads are common holiday foods.**

CHAPTER 7

POLITICS: ANCIENT AND MODERN DEMOCRACIES

Credit for developing democracy goes to the ancient Athenians of the fifth century BCE. The word *democracy* comes from the words *demos*, or "the people," and *kratein*, or "to rule"; democracy means "rule by the people." Adult male Greek citizens could vote in assemblies held 40 times per year. Women, foreigners, males under 18, and slaves were excluded from voting. The basic concept of democracy has since spread all over the world, taking on many different forms.

Today, Greece's government is a parliamentary republic. In this offshoot of democracy, a legislative body elected by the people, known as the parliament, selects the leaders of government. The leaders are chosen according to the popularity of the political parties for which citizens

A Greek man emerges from a voting booth during the June 2012 elections. Democracy's place in Greek culture dates to Athens' Golden Age.

vote in general elections. This means that the government leaders are responsible both to the parliament and to the people, since the people's support is what influences the parliament's choice of leaders. Voting in Greece is required of everyone 18 or older, although this rule is not strictly enforced. Greece has a president, a prime minister, a cabinet, and a parliament. The president is elected by the parliament for a five-year term, and the president chooses the prime minister.

STRUCTURE OF THE GOVERNMENT OF GREECE

Executive	Judicial	Legislative
President

Prime Minister | Supreme Court

The Council of State | Hellenic Parliament |

In Greece, the president is the official head of state but has relatively little power. Instead, the prime minister, who is the head of government, holds executive power in the country. The cabinet consists of the prime minister and a group of other ministers, including the minister for national defense and the minister of state. It is the cabinet's responsibility to decide on the national policies of Greece.

Antonis Samaras was sworn in as prime minister on June 20, 2012.

The current president is Karolos Papoulias. A former minister for foreign affairs, he was first elected to the presidency in 2005. He was reelected for a second five-year term in 2010. He belongs to the Panhellenic Socialist Movement, a center-left political party. On June 17, 2012, legislative elections were held. The center-right New Democracy party won the most seats. After forming a coalition with a few other parties, New Democracy leader Antonis Samaras became the new prime minister on June 20.

A HISTORY OF STRUGGLE

Modern Greece struggled to establish democratic rule. Between World Wars I and II, the country saw contention between those who wanted a monarch as the head of state and those who wanted Greece to be a republic, ruled by the people. Greece was proclaimed a republic in 1923, but a king returned to the throne in 1935.

Greece had seven kings between 1832 and 1973.

Following the end of the civil war between the Communist forces and the National Army in 1949, successive conservative governments ruled Greece. A political leader named Konstantinos Karamanlis played a dominant role between 1955 and 1963. The Greek military junta was in power between 1967 and 1974. In July 1974, Karamanlis returned to power, created a civilian government of national unity, and held elections. The people voted to abolish the monarchy, and Karamanlis's new political party, New Democracy, won the elections. He became prime minister. Greece's parliament elected President Michail Stasinopoulos on December 18, 1974, and approved a new constitution in 1975.

In 2011, a plan known as Kallikratis went into effect, overhauling and simplifying the former political divisions of the country. Where Greece once had 13 regions, 54 prefectures, and 1,034 municipalities, it would now have seven smaller governmental units, 13 regions, and

The current Greek parliament building was once the royal palace.

325 municipalities. This plan was put into place to make municipalities bigger and more powerful, allowing decisions to be made more quickly and efficiently.

PANHELLENIC SOCIALIST MOVEMENT

The Panhellenic Socialist Movement (PASOK) is the social democratic political party of Greece, founded in 1974. It started out as a radical group that called for tighter regulation of Greece's economy and for ending military alliances with other countries. Since then it has become more of a mainstream party. Along with the New Democracy party, it is one of the leading political parties in Greece. PASOK ceased to be the ruling party in 2004, but it still dominates the media and is very vocal. The party suffered major losses in the June 2012 election.

POLITICAL PARTIES

Several political parties, including both liberal (left) and conservative (right) parties, vie for power in Greek elections. New Democracy, Karamanlis's center-right party, has lost support in recent years but regained the voters' confidence in the June 2012 elections. The Democratic Alliance and the Independent Greeks were formed after their leaders left New Democracy. The Panhellenic Socialist Movement, a center-left party, has taken criticism during the recent economic crisis for supporting austerity measures dictated by Western Europe. The Communist Party of Greece is one of Greece's oldest political parties and has a turbulent history,

often refusing to join forces with other leftist parties. The Coalition of the Radical Left is composed of several left-wing parties; it has fought austerity measures, but its attempts to form a coalition with like-minded parties have mostly failed. The Democratic Left was founded by former members of the Coalition of the Radical Left, and the Ecologist Greens focus on environmental issues. Finally, the Popular Orthodox Rally and Golden Dawn parties are right-wing, nationalist, and anti-immigration.

Greece also has several political action groups, including the Civil Servants Confederation (which informs civil servants about their rights and protects them from being exploited in the workplace), the Federation of Greek Industries (which works in the interests of companies in Greece), and the General Confederation of Greek Workers (the largest trade union protecting Greek workers).

UPHOLDING THE LAW

The judicial system in Greece consists of Courts of Ordinary Jurisdiction, which deal with civil and penal cases, and Administrative Courts, which deal with administrative and tax issues and claims against the government. The hierarchy of the Courts of Ordinary Jurisdiction begins with Courts of the Peace on the local level and eventually leads to the Supreme Court. The Administrative Courts include the Administrative Court of First Instance, then the Administrative Court of Appeals, and at the highest level, the Council of State. Just as in the United States, court cases work their way through the hierarchy from the local level to the highest level through the appeals process.

Each of Greece's 13 largest cities has a Court of Appeal.

RELATIONS WITH THE EUROPEAN COMMUNITY

On January 1, 1981, Greece became the tenth member of the European Community, which is now the EU. Greece's foreign relations are similar to those of most other EU countries. It maintains full diplomatic relationships with its neighbors in southeast Europe (except for Macedonia) and has an embassy in the United States, as well as eight consulates in US cities. As a member of NATO, Greece has helped with peacekeeping military missions in Bosnia, Kosovo, and Afghanistan.

Greece has ongoing disagreements with Turkey regarding territorial boundaries in the Aegean Sea, the treatment of Greeks and the Greek Orthodox Church in Istanbul, the treatment of Muslims in Greece, the division of the island of Cyprus into a Greek and a Turkish region,

NAMING DISPUTE

Greece has an ongoing dispute with the country of Macedonia over its name. The country was part of Yugoslavia, but declared its independence in 1991 and became the Republic of Macedonia. However, the Greeks feel the name Macedonia should only be used to refer to their own northern province of the same name. The government even said that it would not officially recognize another state calling itself Macedonia. Many Greeks refer to the country as the "Former Yugoslav Republic of Macedonia (FYROM)" instead. The United Nations is using that same designation until the dispute is settled.

and the large numbers of immigrants who come to Greece illegally from South Asia and the Middle East by way of Turkey. The two countries continue to negotiate in an effort to resolve these issues.

JOINING THE EU

When Greece wanted to join the EU in 1981, it did not meet the economic criteria for membership and had to catch up to the other member states. But Greece also argued that by joining the EU, it would be safeguarding the survival of its then-new democracy. Newly democratic countries formerly belonging to the Soviet Union have used the same argument when requesting to join the EU.

Just as democracy is an important part of Greek politics, so is protest. Thousands in Thessaloníki protested the government's financial policies in 2011.

CHAPTER 8

ECONOMICS: AN ECONOMY IN CRISIS

The future looked bright for Greece at the dawn of the twenty-first century. The country had become part of the European Economic and Monetary Union, and it had a new currency: the euro. Greece's old currency was the drachma, one of the world's oldest coins, which dated from the sixth century BCE. The euro was intended to eliminate fluctuations in exchange rates between European countries that were each using their own currency and create a uniform currency for all of Europe. However, many Greeks associated the euro with a higher cost of living and did not welcome the change.

The word *drachma* means "to grasp."

Tourism is a major sector of Greece's economy.

Euro banknotes and coins

As part of the EU, Greece received funds to modernize and develop its transportation network before the 2004 Summer Olympics in Athens. It built a new airport and finished construction of the city's subway system. Between 1999 and 2007, Greece's economy grew by an average of 4 percent every year, partially because of increased spending by visitors during the Olympics.[1] But the general slowdown of the world economy led to a Greek recession in 2009. Credit was harder to obtain and Greece's budget had a growing deficit, meaning the country was spending more than it took in.

MAKING MONEY IN GREECE

Despite its troubled economy, Greece does have many successful industries. One of the largest industries is tourism; visitors love experiencing Greece's ancient history, its vibrant modern culture, and its climate. More than 18 percent of Greece's gross domestic product (GDP) comes from the tourism industry.[2]

Other important industries include shipping, food processing, tobacco, textiles, chemicals, medicine, cement, glass, and heavy equipment. Agriculture—including crops such as wheat, corn, barley, sugar beets, olives, tomatoes, wine, potatoes, and cotton—was once a major component of Greece's economy, but it has become less important over the past ten years and now represents only 3 percent of the GDP.[3] Greece's biggest trading partners are other nations of the EU, but it also trades

Germany is Greece's largest export and import partner.

with countries such as China and Russia. Greece imports more than it exports, resulting in a trade deficit: the country spends US$64.5 billion on imported goods and services, but exports only US$22 billion worth of goods to other countries.[4] The strong tourism and shipping industries no longer make up the difference.

Greece had an unemployment rate over 21 percent in early 2012.[5] Almost 5 million people were part of the labor force, with most of them working in services, followed by industry and then agriculture.[6] One of the stipulations the EU placed on Greece as a condition of loans and bailout money was that the government needed to become more effective in collecting income tax. A Greek worker must make more than 12,000 euros a year in order to pay income tax, but documents released by the Greek government in 2008 showed that many

FISHING AND AQUACULTURE

Many Greeks living on the coast or on the islands once earned their living by fishing. They used open boats with a single mast called *caiques*. Often entire families would work together to fish. Today fish farming, also called aquaculture, has become a large industry; most of it is conducted using large sea cages, but some types of fish are farmed in special lagoons. The aquaculture industry has also resulted in the colonization of otherwise uninhabited islands.

Whether for shipping, fishing boats, or cruise ships, the sea is very important to the Greek economy.

Resources of Greece

workers were not truthfully reporting their income and thus were avoiding paying income tax. Tax evasion has become rampant in the upper levels of Greek society as well. The Greek government has only recently managed to enforce laws and procedures to collect the high property taxes it established as another way to reduce the nation's rising debt.

MONEY TROUBLES

Greece's economy shrank 2.3 percent in 2009. It contracted by a further 3.5 percent in 2010, and continued its downward spiral with a 6 percent loss in 2011.[7] Finally, the situation became so critical that credit agencies downgraded Greece's international debt rating, indicating the increased risk of investing in the country. The downgrade shook confidence in the nation's economic future. Public finances were getting worse, the government's financial statistics were being misreported or were inaccurate, and the country was not keeping up with the reforms it had promised to enact. As a result, the International Monetary Fund and the EU gave Greece emergency loans to bail it out of its financial crisis. It was feared that if Greece's economy sank much further, it could have a negative effect on the other EU countries or even on the world economy.

Greece has received more than $300 billion in bailout money.

In exchange for the bailout, the Greek government agreed to huge spending cuts, drastic reforms, increased tax collection, and restricted healthcare spending to help its economy recover. However, many

DOING BUSINESS IN GREECE

Many Western countries see Greece as an ideal location to do business. Its geographic location makes it a good base for companies that want to expand into the Balkans, Turkey, and the Middle East. People native to the area also tend to have a better understanding of those cultures and how they work, which helps Western companies to negotiate and undertake business transactions and partnerships. For this reason, these companies also recruit Greek businessmen and entrepreneurs. The recent economic crisis, however, is changing this picture, and it remains unclear what the future holds for the Greek business landscape.

investors are skeptical that Greece can do all these things when its economic outlook remains bleak, the public is unhappy, and the political leadership is unstable.

After the Greek parliament passed further economic austerity measures in February 2012, there were widespread protests and riots in the streets, especially in the center of Athens. The measures included eliminating 15,000 jobs and reducing the minimum wage by 20 percent, as well as the cutting of pensions. Prime Minister Loukas Papadimos condemned the riots, saying that "vandalism, violence and destruction have no place in a democratic country and won't be tolerated." He added that the measures

A man yells at riot police during protests of Greek's austerity measures in May 2011. The parliament building stands in the background.

ALBANIAN IMMIGRATION

One of the biggest immigration problems for Greece has been an influx of illegal immigrants from Albania. They began arriving after the collapse of the Soviet Union in 1991. Hundreds of thousands of Albanians, most of them unskilled, have entered Greece. Many Greeks claim the Albanians have brought with them a level of crime that their country has not experienced before. Immigrants in general have long supplied Greece with cheap labor, but they became less welcome when Greece's unemployment levels began to rise.

would "set the foundations for the reform and recovery of the economy."[8]

Greeks are protesting more than just the state of their economy and the measures being taken to fix it. At a time when unemployment is high and government aid money is decreasing, many Greeks also protest the presence of immigrants, both legal and illegal. Greece now accounts for 90 percent of the illegal border crossings in the EU because it is a gateway from many immigrants' home countries to what they see as a better life in Western Europe. Greece created a border patrol to prevent illegal immigrants from entering the country, but the number of immigrants has proven too great to handle. In one eight-mile (12.5 km) portion of the border, the European border management agency noted that more than 30,000 illegal crossings were reported from January to September 2010.[9]

However, there are protests on both sides of the issue: some Greeks denounce the presence of so many immigrants whom they see as a threat to employment and a drain on Greece's resources, while others protest against what they see as racism and inhumane treatment of immigrants.

Greece's far-right Golden Dawn party has called for placing landmines to counter immigration.

CHAPTER 9
GREECE TODAY

A Greek word for work, *douleia*, originally meant slavery or work that is heavy and unrewarding. Some of these connotations are still present in many people's attitudes towards work—family comes first in Greece, and people usually work to live rather than live to work. Large retailers typically do not open until 9:00 a.m. and are closed on Saturday afternoons and Sundays, though extended hours are often followed in tourist areas. Offices are always closed on the weekend.

During the hot summer season, many Greeks take a siesta in the late afternoon, which is the time to nap or relax. Many businesses and offices close in the early afternoon for siesta, and some businesses then reopen for evening shopping hours. For the most part, life

The term *siesta* comes from Spanish. Afternoon naps are common in many cultures.

Greek kids march in the annual celebration of Greek independence.

comes to a stop for several hours each afternoon, resuming in the cooler evening hours. It is not unusual to eat dinner after 9:00 p.m.

When they aren't in school, Greek teens like to hang out with their group of friends (called a *parea*, or company) at coffee shops, cafeterias, and shopping centers. They talk about school, music, and friends, just like teens everywhere. Because of Greece's high unemployment rate, many do not have a part-time job. The minimum age for employment in Greece is 15, and teens aged 15–18 must have a special "work book" from the Department of Labor. It lists the workers' jobs, the hours they work, and their medical exams. It is meant to keep teens from working in dangerous or unsafe jobs. Teens still in school can work up to six hours a day or a total of 30 hours a week. Many teens work as servers in cafes or bars.

Greek society is very family-oriented. Greek families often include grandparents, parents,

SMALL BUSINESSES

Among the hardest hit areas of the Greek economy under the present economic conditions are the small, often family-owned businesses. Most of these businesses have 50 or fewer employees, but they make up 99 percent of businesses and employ three-quarters of the non-government-employed workforce.[1] Many have been forced to fire employees or even close.

Three Greek teens walk through Athens. Greece's high unemployment rate has meant that many teens cannot find jobs.

children, and sometimes aunts and uncles all living in the same household or in adjacent apartments. Many Greeks desire to live in the same house as their children and their parents, and Greek parents often try to buy a nearby house or apartment for their daughters.

In 2012, 18.7 percent of Greek parliament members were women.

Women in Greece tend to run their households, since life is so family-based. However, unlike other European and Western cultures, women are generally not heavily involved in politics or economic decision-making. Greater numbers of younger women have joined the professional workforce than in past generations, but they still face challenges in the workplace in promotion and job advancement.

EDUCATION

Education is very important to the Greeks, and 96 percent of those over the age of 15 can read and write. Kids must attend primary school between the ages of six and 12, and then spend three years at a *gymnasium*, which is for pupils aged 13 to 15. Then they go on to the *lyceum*, which is high school. Education is free, but some Greek families also send their children to additional lessons or to private tutors, especially for subjects such as English or other foreign languages, in order

Greek youths march in remembrance of the 1973 student protests against the military junta.

BRAIN DRAIN

A major problem facing Greece, especially in difficult economic times, is something known as "brain drain." Many young, smart, skilled professionals are leaving the country for other parts of the world where they can earn better salaries and find advanced training opportunities. Those who stay and work in Greece are often poorly paid and heavily taxed, if they can find jobs at all. The Greek educational system has also not kept up with the rest of the modern world. According to a 2012 article in the *Economist*:

> The most destructive brain drain is of the young. Since 2008, ever more young people (mostly in their 20s) have gone, often to foreign universities. "When I left to study abroad in 2006 I was the odd man out," says a young Greek lawyer. "Now I thank my lucky stars." Greece's archaic education system and strikes have held back those who pursued their education at home. Exams have been delayed or cancelled. Some students are a year or more behind in their studies.[2]

to help them succeed in the college entrance exams that decide who gets into which school.

For teens approaching the end of high school, continuing to higher education is common, especially since state colleges and universities in Greece are also free. Students can either attend a regular university or a vocational school. However, with so many students wanting to go to college, and with more applicants than openings, privately run schools called *frontistiria* are thriving. These schools prepare students to take the university entrance

Immigrants and children of immigrants protest for their rights in Athens in 2007. Immigration policies present one of Greece's major challenges moving forward.

exams. One year of military service is also required of all Greek men when they turn 18, but if they are going on to higher education, that service can be deferred until a later date.

CHALLENGING TIMES

Due to the troubled economy of Greece, the financial cutbacks it is being forced to make, and the high unemployment rate, it is a challenging time for many Greeks. Many resent that the European Union is overseeing their country's affairs and dictating austerity measures as a condition of receiving aid and loans. The EU considered taking over the management of Greece's budget, and many of the EU countries have indicated that they are losing patience with Greece and the continued need for bailouts. There is also concern that Greece will default on its loans despite the measures it has taken to improve the economy. Economic concerns are compounded with concerns about whether the large influx of immigrants is serving to help or hinder Greece's economy.

In 2012, it was projected that Greece could leave the euro if its economic issues continued.

At the same time, Greece continues to experience issues with water pollution and threats to the environment. Because the country has long been trying to achieve the same economic success as the rest of the EU, it has neglected the environmental impact of tourism, industrialization, development, and intensive agriculture. According to a report on Greece's environmental problems:

Greece's environment faces some major environmental challenges, such as air emissions from transport and electricity power stations, overexploitation of its water resources, water pollution, degradation of its coastal zones, loss of biodiversity in terrestrial and marine ecosystems and increasing municipal and industrial waste.[3]

As with any modern country, Greece must balance the need to be economically strong as part of a larger group—in this case, the EU—with the needs of its people. However, the Greeks are fiercely proud of their country and their heritage. Greece has an incredibly vast cultural history, thousands of years old and boasting the roots of democracy and philosophy, as well as a wealth of poetry, prose, theater, and myth that is part of the world's literary heritage. As the Greeks move forward, working to repair

THE GREEK NATIONAL ANTHEM

The Greek National Anthem, called "Hymn to Liberty," is actually the longest national anthem in the world, consisting of 158 stanzas! But today it is almost always performed in a shortened version with just two stanzas. Translated into English, they are:

*I shall always recognize you
by the dreadful sword you hold
as the Earth with searching vision
you survey with spirit bold*

*From the Greeks of old whose dying
brought to life and spirit free
now with ancient valour rising
let us hail you, oh Liberty![4]*

"The beginning is the most important part of any work."[5]

—*Plato,* The Republic

their nation and restore its place of prominence, they can continue to draw strength from their rich past as they face the challenges of the future.

The Greek people can look to their past for inspiration as they tackle the twenty-first century problems they now face.

TIMELINE

3000 BCE	The Minoans and Mycenaeans begin colonizing Greece.
1600 BCE	The Santorini volcano erupts, likely causing the decline of the Minoan civilization.
1150 BCE	Greek invasions from the north overrun the Mycenaeans.
776 BCE	The first Olympic Games take place.
700–480 BCE	The Greek city-states consolidate their power and colonize other regions of the Mediterranean.
480–431 BCE	Following a victory in the Persian Wars, Athens experiences its Golden Age.
338 BCE	Philip II of Macedon conquers Greece.
ca. 400–1453 CE	The Byzantine Empire, and its influence over Greece, rises and falls.
1453	The Ottoman Turks capture Constantinople and establish control over the Greek lands.
1821	Greeks launch their War of Independence.
1830	Greece is recognized as an independent nation.
1896	The first modern Olympic Games are held in Athens.

1922	The Asia Minor Disaster occurs, resulting in an influx of thousands of refugees to Greece.
1941	Greece is invaded and occupied by Nazi Germany.
1944	Greece is liberated from the Nazis.
1946–1949	The Greek government forces defeat the Communists in the Greek Civil War.
1967–1974	The military junta controls Greece.
1974	The junta collapses; Greece abolishes the monarchy and becomes a democratic republic.
1975	A new Greek constitution is enacted.
1981	Greece joins the European Union.
1999	Earthquakes rock Turkey and Greece less than a month apart.
2004	The Olympic Games are held in Athens again.
2009	Greece's economy begins to shrink, austerity measures are taken, and citizens riot in the streets.
2011	Kallikratis goes into effect, simplifying Greece's regional divisions.

FACTS AT YOUR FINGERTIPS

GEOGRAPHY

Official Name: Hellenic Republic

Area: 50,949 square miles (131,957 sq km)

Climate: temperate; mild, wet winters and hot, dry summers

Highest elevation: Mount Olympus, 9,570 feet (2,917 meters) above sea level

Lowest elevation: Mediterranean Sea, 0 feet (0 m) above sea level

Significant geographic features: Mount Olympus

PEOPLE

Population (July 2011 est.): 10,767,827

Most populous city: Athens

Ethnic groups: Greeks, Turks, Macedonian Slavs, Albanians, Armenians, Bulgarians, Jews, and Vlachs

Percentage of residents living in urban areas: 61 percent

Life expectancy: 80.05 years (world rank: 31)

Language: Greek

Religion(s): Greek Orthodox, 98 percent; some Muslim, Catholic, Protestant, and Jewish

GOVERNMENT AND ECONOMY

Government: parliamentary republic

Capital: Athens

Date of adoption of current constitution: 1975

Head of state: president

Head of government: prime minister

Legislature: Hellenic Parliament

Currency: euro

Industries and natural resources: lignite, petroleum, iron ore, bauxite, lead, zinc, nickel, magnesite, marble, salt, hydropower potential

NATIONAL SYMBOLS

Holidays: Independence Day, March 25. Polytechneio Day, November 17.

Flag: nine equal horizontal stripes of blue alternating with white, and a blue square bearing a white cross appears in the upper left corner. The cross symbolizes Greek Orthodox, the established religion of the country.

National symbol: the Greek Cross (a white cross on a blue background with arms of equal length)

National Anthem: "Hymn to Liberty"

National Animal: dolphin

KEY PEOPLE

Pericles led Athens during its Golden Age in the fifth century BCE.

Otto of Greece (1815–1867) was the first king of modern Greece after the Greek War of Independence.

Konstantinos Karamanlis (1907–1998) was a famous Greek politician who helped restore democracy in 1974 following the seven-year military junta.

REGIONS OF GREECE (REGION; CAPITAL)

Mount Athos (self-governed region)

Eastern Macedonia and Thrace; Komotiní

Attica; Athens

Western Greece; Patras

Western Macedonia; Kozáni

Ionian Islands; Corfu

Epirus; Ioánnina

Central Macedonia; Thessaloníki

Crete; Iráklion

South Aegean; Hermoúpolis

Peloponnese; Trípolis

Central Greece; Lamía

Thessaly; Lárissa

North Aegean; Mytilene

GLOSSARY

acid rain
Rain caused by pollution that can damage plants and animals.

austerity
Reducing budget deficits by cutting spending drastically and increasing taxes.

baklava
A pastry filled with chopped nuts, sweetened with honey or syrup.

epic poem
A long narrative poem that tells of historical or legendary heroes and events.

fascist
An extremely nationalist form of government with expansionist and often racist tendencies.

gross domestic product
A measure of a country's economy; the total of all goods and services produced in a country in a year.

guerilla fighter
A soldier not in an organized army, usually fighting a larger force.

industrialization
The transformation of a society from one based on farming to one based on manufacturing.

loam

A fertile soil containing clay and sand.

military junta

A government led by a group of military dictators.

monotheistic

Believing in one god.

pankration

A martial art with almost no rules that was introduced in ancient Greece.

polytheism

The belief in multiple gods.

sultan

A Muslim ruler of the Ottoman Empire.

terra rosa

Red clay soil produced by the weathering of limestone.

ADDITIONAL RESOURCES

SELECTED BIBLIOGRAPHY

Buhayer, Constantine. *Culture Smart! Greece.* New York: Kuperard, 2010. Print.

Clogg, Richard. *A Concise History of Greece, Second Edition.* New York: Cambridge, 2010. Print.

Dubin, Marc. *DK Eyewitness Travel: Greece: Athens and the Mainland.* New York: DK, 2011. Print.

FURTHER READINGS

Adkins, Lesley and Roy A. Adkins. *Handbook to Life in Ancient Greece.* New York: Facts on File, 2005. Print.

Hamby, Zachary. *Mythology for Teens: Classic Myths for Today's World.* Austin, TX: Prufrock Press, 2009. Print.

Leontis, Artemis. *Culture and Customs of Greece.* Westport, CT: Greenwood Press, 2009. Print.

WEB LINKS

To learn more about Greece, visit ABDO Publishing Company online at **www.abdopublishing.com**. Web sites about Greece are featured on our Book Links page. These links are routinely monitored and updated to provide the most current information available.

PLACES TO VISIT

If you are ever in Greece, check out these important and interesting sites!

The Acropolis, Athens

Visit the Parthenon and other ancient Greek temples, as well as the new Acropolis Museum.

Ancient Olympia

Visit the site of the first Olympics, as well as an archaeological museum dedicated to the history of the games with a model of how the site originally looked.

Corfu

See one of Greece's most beautiful islands, with a fortress built by the Venetians, museums, and beaches.

Delphi

The site of the most sacred place in ancient Greece features a museum about Delphi and the oracle.

SOURCE NOTES

CHAPTER 1. A VISIT TO GREECE

1. "Secrets of the Parthenon." *NOVA*. PBS, 29 January 2008. Web. 2 Aug. 2012.

2. "The World Factbook: Greece." *Central Intelligence Agency.* Central Intelligence Agency, 26 July 2012. Web. 2 Aug. 2012.

3. Percy Bysshe Shelley. *Hellas.* London, 1886. *Google Book Search*. Web. 2 Aug. 2012.

CHAPTER 2. GEOGRAPHY: A LAND OF SEAS AND MOUNTAINS

1. "The World Factbook: Greece." *Central Intelligence Agency.* Central Intelligence Agency, 26 July 2012. Web. 2 Aug. 2012.

2. Ibid.

3. "Background Note: Greece." *US Department of State.* US Department of State, 22 March 2012. Web. 2 Aug. 2012.

4. Ibid.

5. "The World Factbook: Greece." *Central Intelligence Agency.* Central Intelligence Agency, 26 July 2012. Web. 2 Aug. 2012.

6. "Greece." *Encyclopædia Britannica.* Encyclopaedia Britannica, 2012. Web. 2 Aug. 2012.

7. "Greece." *Weatherbase.* Canty and Associates, 2012. Web. 2 Aug. 2012.

8. "Europe: Highest Temperature." *World Weather/Climate Extremes Archive.* World Meteorological Organization, n.d. Web. 2 Aug. 2012.

CHAPTER 3. ANIMALS AND NATURE: ENVIRONMENT AT RISK

1. "The Olive Tree and Olive Oil." *Sfakia-Crete.* World2C Media, 18 July 2011. Web. 2 Aug. 2012.

2. "Polluted Concrete Coastline No Lure for Greeks." *Sydney Morning Herald.* Reuters, 17 October 2007. Web. 2 Aug. 2012.

3. "Summary Statistics: Summaries by Country, Table 5, Threatened Species in Each Country." *IUCN Red List of Threatened Species.* International Union for Conservation of Nature and Natural Resources, 2011. Web. 2 Aug. 2012.

4. "Olympus National Park." *National Geographic Travel.* National Geographic Society, n.d. Web. 2. Aug. 2012.

CHAPTER 4. HISTORY: LAND OF THE ANCIENTS

1. Alfred North Whitehead. *Process and Reality.* New York, 1929. *Google Book Search.* Web. 2 Aug. 2012.

CHAPTER 5. PEOPLE: GREEK PRIDE

1. "The World Factbook: Greece." *Central Intelligence Agency.* Central Intelligence Agency, 26 July 2012. Web. 2 Aug. 2012.

2. Ibid.

3. Ibid.

4. "The World Factbook: The United States." *Central Intelligence Agency.* Central Intelligence Agency, 26 July 2012. Web. 2 Aug. 2012.

5. "The World Factbook: Greece." *Central Intelligence Agency.* Central Intelligence Agency, 26 July 2012. Web. 2 Aug. 2012.

6. Ibid.

SOURCE NOTES CONTINUED

CHAPTER 6. CULTURE: HOME OF THE OLYMPICS

None.

CHAPTER 7. POLITICS: ANCIENT AND MODERN DEMOCRACIES

None.

CHAPTER 8. ECONOMICS: AN ECONOMY IN CRISIS

1. "Background Note: Greece." *US Department of State*. US Department of State, 22 March 2012. Web. 2 Aug. 2012.

2. *Tourism in OECD Countries 2008: Trends and Policies*. Organization for Economic Cooperation and Development, 2008. Print. 137.

3. "Background Note: Greece." *US Department of State*. US Department of State, 22 March 2012. Web. 2 Aug. 2012.

4. Ibid.

5. "The World Factbook: Greece." *Central Intelligence Agency*. Central Intelligence Agency, 26 July 2012. Web. 2 Aug. 2012.

6. "Background Note: Greece." *US Department of State*. US Department of State, 22 March 2012. Web. 2 Aug. 2012.

7. "The World Factbook: Greece." *Central Intelligence Agency*. Central Intelligence Agency, 26 July 2012. Web. 2 Aug. 2012.

8. "Greece MPs Pass Austerity Plan Amid Violent Protests." *BBC News*. BBC, 13 Feb. 2012. Web. 2 Aug. 2012.

9. Elena Becatoros. "Greece: Europe's Gateway for Illegal Immigration." *Washington Post*. Associated Press, 4 Nov. 2010. Web. 2 Aug. 2012.

CHAPTER 9. GREECE TODAY

1. "The Mediterranean Blues." *Economist*. Economist, 14 Jan. 2012. Web. 2 Aug. 2012.

2. Ibid.

3. Athanasios Valavanidis and Thomais Vlachogianni. "The Most Important and Urgent Environmental Problems in Greece in the Last Decade (2000-2010)." Department of Chemistry, University of Athens, 18 Mar. 2011. Web. 2 Aug. 2012.

4. "Greece." *London 2012*. The Telegraph, n.d. Web. 2 Aug. 2012.

5. Plato. *The Republic*. Trans. Benjamin Jowett. London, 1894. *Google Book Search*. Web. 2 Aug. 2012.

INDEX

PHOTO CREDITS